I WANT TO TR

Learn How To Build A Strong and Lasting Connection With Your Partner

By

Stephanie Rucker

Copyright © Stephanie Rucker

All right reserved

TABLE OF CONTENT

LEARN HOW TO BUILD A STRONG AND LASTING CONNECTION WITH YOUR PARTNER 1

UNDERSTANDING TRUST 6

THE IMPORTANCE OF COMMUNICATION 12

CONSISTENCY AND RELIABILITY 18

CREATING A SAFE SPACE FOR VULNERABILITY 24

DEALING WITH BETRAYAL 30

KEY ACTIONS TO BUILDING TRUST IN A ROMANTIC RELATIONSHIP: .. 36

INTRODUCTION

Building trust between lovers is crucial for maintaining a healthy and fulfilling relationship. Understanding and meeting each other's needs and goals need open and honest communication, which is only possible when there is trust between the parties. Additionally, trust gives one the ability to be open and honest without worrying about being judged or rejected. This book offers advice on how to establish trust between lovers, including how to speak, be open, and create a secure environment for vulnerability. Couples may strengthen and deepen their relationship by heeding the recommendations in this book.

Trust is the foundation of any strong and lasting relationship. It takes time and effort to build, but once established, it can withstand the test of time. Trust is not something that can be earned overnight; it is built over time through consistent actions and behaviours.

To build trust between lovers, it is important to establish open and honest communication. This means being willing to listen and hear each other's perspectives, sharing your feelings, and being transparent about your thoughts and actions. It also means being willing to compromise and work through any conflicts that may arise.

Another key aspect of building trust is being consistent in your behaviour. This means being reliable, dependable, and keeping your word. It also means being true to your feelings and intentions and not being afraid to be vulnerable and share your deepest thoughts and feelings with your partner.

Creating a safe space for vulnerability is also important for building trust. This means being supportive and non-judgmental of each other and being willing to offer a listening ear and a shoulder to lean on. It also means being willing to forgive and move past any mistakes or misunderstandings that may occur.

CHAPTER ONE

Understanding Trust

The first step in building trust in a romantic relationship understands what trust is and why it's important. In this chapter, we will explore the definition of trust and how it plays a role in creating a strong and healthy relationship.

What is trust? Trust is defined as a belief in the reliability, truth, ability, or strength of someone or something. In a romantic relationship, trust is about feeling secure and confident in your partner's words and actions.

Trust is a vital component of any successful romantic relationship. It serves as the cornerstone upon which all other facets of a relationship, such as love, intimacy, and commitment, are constructed. Without trust, a relationship is more likely to fail, resulting in anger, envy, and feelings of insecurity. We will discuss the value of trust in romantic relationships in this chapter, as well as present the main ideas and techniques that will be discussed in this manual on how to develop trust between lovers.

Types of Trust

Different types of trust play a role in a romantic relationship, including:

Trust in Character: This type of trust is about believing that your partner is honest, dependable, and has your best interests at heart.

Trust in Competence: This type of trust is about believing that your partner is competent in their actions.

Trust in Communication: This type of trust is about believing that your partner will listen to you and be truthful in their words.

Why is Trust Important in Romantic Relationships?

Trust is the glue that holds a relationship together. It allows for open and honest communication, which is essential for understanding and addressing each other's needs and wants. Trust also allows for the freedom to be vulnerable and to share one's deepest feelings without fear of judgment or rejection. When trust is present in a relationship, partners feel safe and secure, which leads to deeper levels of intimacy and connection.

On the other hand, a lack of trust can lead to feelings of insecurity, jealousy, and resentment. When trust is broken, it can be difficult to regain, and a relationship may never fully recover. Trust is not something that can be earned overnight; it is built over time through consistent actions and behaviours.

Key Concepts and Strategies for Building Trust

This guide will provide tips and strategies for building trust between lovers, including ways to communicate effectively, be transparent, and create a safe space for vulnerability. By following the advice in this guide, couples can strengthen their bond and deepen their connection.

Effective Communication: Open and honest communication is essential for building trust. This means being willing to listen and hear each other's perspectives, share your feelings, and be transparent about your thoughts and actions.

Transparency: Being transparent and honest in your actions and behaviour is crucial for building trust. This means being reliable, dependable, and keeping your word. It also means being true to your feelings and intentions and not being afraid to be vulnerable and share your deepest thoughts and feelings with your partner.

Creating a Safe Space for Vulnerability:

Creating a safe space for vulnerability is also important for building trust. This means being supportive and non-judgmental of each other and being willing to offer a listening ear and a shoulder to lean on. It also means being willing to forgive and move past any mistakes or misunderstandings that may occur.

In conclusion, trust is an essential component of any successful romantic relationship. By establishing open and honest communication, being consistent in their behaviour, and creating a safe space for vulnerability, couples can strengthen their bond and deepen their connection. This guide will provide tips and strategies for building trust between lovers and helping couples create a strong foundation for their relationships.

CHAPTER TWO

The Importance of Communication

Effective communication is a key aspect of building trust between lovers. It allows partners to understand and address each other's needs and wants and to share their thoughts and feelings openly and honestly. In this chapter, we will delve deeper into the importance of open and honest communication in building trust between lovers and explore the different types of communication that are essential for maintaining trust in a relationship.

Effective communication is not only about expressing one's thoughts, feelings, and needs but also about understanding and acknowledging the perspective of the other person. This means that both partners should be willing to listen, hear, and validate each other's feelings and thoughts.

Another important aspect of communication is setting boundaries and speaking up when something is bothering or hurting someone. This means being assertive and clear when expressing what one wants, needs, and expects. Allowing one's feelings to fester or bottling them up can lead to resentment and mistrust.

Effective communication also includes non-verbal cues and body language, which can convey a lot of meaning. For example, eye contact, facial expressions, and physical touch can communicate trust, love, and affection. Additionally, using "I" statements instead of "you" statements can help avoid blame and defensiveness and encourage more productive and understanding conversations.

Additionally, it is also important to have regular check-ins with your partner to discuss the state of the relationship, what's working, and what's not. This allows couples to address issues and conflicts proactively before they become bigger problems. It also allows couples to communicate their expectations, needs, and wants, so they can work together to ensure that they are met.

The Importance of Active Listening

Active listening is the act of fully listening and paying attention to what your partner is saying. It involves not only hearing the words but also understanding their underlying meaning and emotions. Active listening is essential for building trust because it shows your partner that you value their thoughts and feelings and that you are genuinely interested in what they have to say.

Sharing Feelings

Sharing your feelings and thoughts with your partner is an important aspect of building trust. It allows your partner to understand you on a deeper level and see things from your perspective. It also allows you to be vulnerable and share your deepest thoughts and feelings without fear of judgment or rejection. This level of vulnerability helps create deeper levels of intimacy and connection.

Being Transparent

Being transparent and honest in your actions and behaviour is crucial for building trust. This means being reliable, dependable, and keeping your word. It also means being true to your feelings and intentions and not being afraid to be vulnerable and share your deepest thoughts and feelings with your partner. When your partner knows that they can trust you and rely on you, they will feel more secure in the relationship.

Compromise and Conflict Resolution

Compromise and conflict resolution are also important aspects of building trust. When conflicts arise, it is important to address them promptly, be willing to compromise and find a solution that works for both partners. Avoiding conflicts or sweeping them under the rug will only lead to a build-up of resentment and mistrust.

In summary, effective communication is a key aspect of building trust between lovers. It allows for open and honest dialogue, active listening, sharing feelings, and being transparent. It also involves understanding, validating, and acknowledging each other's perspectives; setting boundaries; being assertive and clear; and using non-verbal cues and body language. Regular check-ins, which allow couples to address issues and conflicts proactively, are also important for maintaining a healthy and successful relationship.

CHAPTER THREE

Consistency and Reliability

Consistency and reliability are essential for building trust between lovers. Your partner will feel more secure in the relationship if they know they can rely on you and trust in your actions. In this chapter, we will discuss the importance of being consistent and reliable in building trust between lovers and explore how keeping your word and being dependable can establish trust and build a sense of security in a relationship.

Consistency and reliability include being consistent in your actions and words and not sending mixed signals. When there is a disconnection between what one says and what one does, it can create confusion, uncertainty, and mistrust.

Additionally, consistency and reliability also mean being accountable for your actions and taking responsibility for any mistakes or misunderstandings that may occur. This means owning up to one's actions, apologizing when necessary and making amends to repair any damage that may have been caused.

It also means being consistent in one's values, principles, and beliefs and standing by them; this will give your partner a sense of trust, knowing that you are consistent in your actions.

Consistency and reliability also mean being consistent in the level of effort and energy put into the relationship. A relationship requires time, energy, and effort to maintain and grow. When both partners are consistent in this effort, it creates trust and security.

Keeping Your Word

Keeping your word and following through on your commitments is essential for building trust between lovers. When your partner knows that they can rely on you to keep your promises, they will feel more secure in the relationship. This means being dependable, following through on plans, being on time, and being honest about your intentions and actions.

Being Consistent in Your Behaviour

Being consistent in your behaviour is also important for building trust. This means being the same person in every situation and not being swayed by outside influences. It also means being honest and true to yourself and not pretending to be someone you're not. When your partner knows that they can trust you to act in a certain way, they will feel more secure in the relationship.

Being Vulnerable and Honest

Being vulnerable and honest with your partner is an important aspect of building trust. This means being open and transparent about your feelings, thoughts, and intentions. It also means being willing to share your deepest thoughts and feelings without fear of judgment or rejection. When your partner knows that they can trust you to be honest and vulnerable, they will feel more connected and intimate with you.

In summary, consistency and reliability are essential for building trust between lovers. It includes keeping one's word, being consistent in one's behaviour, being honest and vulnerable, and being accountable for one's actions. It also includes being consistent in one's values, principles, and beliefs and putting consistent effort into the relationship. When both partners are consistent and reliable, it creates trust and security, which leads to deeper levels of intimacy and connection.

CHAPTER FOUR

Creating a Safe Space for Vulnerability

Creating a safe space for vulnerability is an important aspect of building trust between lovers. It allows partners to share their deepest thoughts and feelings without fear of judgment or rejection. In this chapter, we will delve into the importance of creating a safe space for vulnerability in building trust between lovers and explore how being supportive and non-judgmental of each other and being willing to offer a listening ear and a shoulder to lean on can create a deeper level of trust and intimacy.

Creating a safe space for vulnerability also means creating an environment where both partners feel comfortable expressing their emotions. This can be achieved by setting clear boundaries and rules where both partners feel safe to express their emotions without fear of judgment or rejection. This means being respectful of each other's boundaries and being willing to listen to and support each other.

It also means creating a space where both partners feel comfortable expressing their vulnerabilities without fear of being judged or rejected. This includes being willing to discuss sensitive topics, such as past traumas, fears, and insecurities. When partners feel safe to be vulnerable, it creates a deeper sense of intimacy and trust.

It's also important to note that creating a safe space for vulnerability is a continuous process. It requires effort and work from both partners. This means that both partners need to be willing to put in the time and effort to create and maintain a safe space for vulnerability. It also means being willing to have difficult conversations and address any issues or concerns that may arise.

Creating a safe space for vulnerability is an important aspect of building trust between lovers. It allows partners to share their deepest thoughts and feelings without fear of judgment or rejection. By being supportive and non-judgmental of each other, and being willing to offer a listening ear and a shoulder to lean on, couples can create a deeper level of trust and intimacy. Creating a safe space for vulnerability also involves setting clear boundaries, being respectful of each other's boundaries, being willing to listen and support each other and being willing to put in the time and effort to create and maintain a safe space for vulnerability.

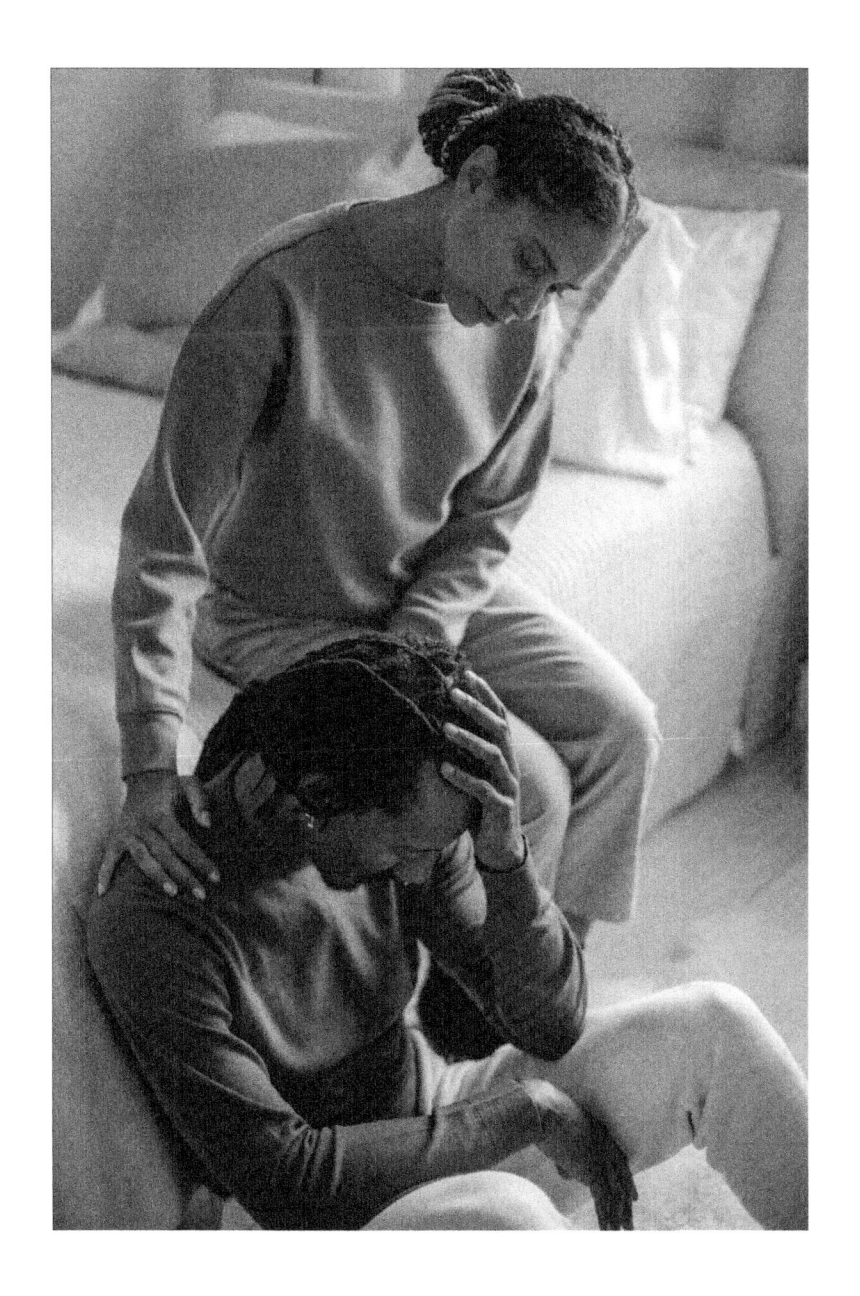

Being Supportive and Non-Judgmental

Being supportive and non-judgmental of each other is essential for creating a safe space for vulnerability. This means being willing to listen, hear each other's perspectives, and offer a listening ear and a shoulder to lean on. It also means being willing to validate each other's feelings and offer words of encouragement and support. When your partner knows that they can be vulnerable and that they will be met with understanding and support, they will feel more comfortable sharing their deepest thoughts and feelings.

Creating a Safe Space for Sharing

Creating a safe space for sharing also means being willing to share your thoughts and feelings. This means being vulnerable and transparent about your thoughts and feelings and being willing to share your struggles and challenges. This level of vulnerability creates a deeper level of trust and intimacy, as it allows both partners to understand each other on a deeper level.

Forgiveness and Moving Forward

Forgiveness is also an important aspect of creating a safe space for vulnerability. This means being willing to let go of past mistakes and misunderstandings and moving forward with a renewed sense of trust and understanding. When your partner knows that they can make mistakes and that they will be forgiven, they will feel more comfortable being vulnerable and sharing their thoughts and feelings.

In conclusion, creating a safe space for vulnerability is an important aspect of building trust between lovers. It allows partners to share their deepest thoughts and feelings without fear of judgment or rejection. By being supportive and non-judgmental of each other, and being willing to offer a listening ear and a shoulder to lean on, couples can create a deeper level of trust and intimacy. Forgiveness and moving forward also play a role in creating a safe space for vulnerability and maintaining trust in a relationship.

CHAPTER FIVE

Dealing with Betrayal

Despite our best efforts, trust can still be broken in a romantic relationship. In this chapter, we will discuss how to deal with betrayal and rebuild trust after it has been broken.

The Impact of Betrayal

Betrayal can be devastating in a romantic relationship. It can cause feelings of hurt, anger, and disappointment. Betrayal can also shake the foundation of trust and make it difficult to feel confident and secure in the relationship moving forward.

Steps for Dealing with Betrayal

If trust has been broken in your relationship, here are some steps you can take to heal and rebuild trust:

Take time to process: Allow yourself time to process your feelings and emotions before discussing the situation with your partner.

Communicate openly: Have an open and honest conversation with your partner about what happened, how you feel, and what you need from them.

Identify the root cause: Try to understand why the betrayal occurred and what can be done to prevent it from happening again in the future.

Be willing to forgive: Forgiveness is a process, and it may take time to get there. But to move forward, both partners must be willing to forgive and work on rebuilding trust.

Establish clear boundaries: Clearly define what behaviours are and are not acceptable in the relationship moving forward.

Seek outside help: If necessary, consider seeking the help of a therapist or counsellor to support you through the healing process.

Betrayal can be a difficult and painful experience, but it is possible to rebuild trust in a romantic relationship. By communicating openly, identifying the root cause, and working together to establish clear boundaries, you can move past the betrayal and build a stronger, more trusting relationship. With patience, understanding, and commitment, you can rebuild trust and create a relationship that is more fulfilling, meaningful, and enjoyable.

Maintaining Trust in Difficult Times

Building trust takes time and effort, and it's important to remember that trust is not something that can be earned overnight. Even in the most secure relationships, trust can be tested during difficult times. It's important to remember that trust is a continuous process and requires effort to maintain. This means being willing to work through difficulties together and continue to communicate openly and honestly, even during difficult times.

In conclusion, trust is an essential component of any successful romantic relationship. By establishing open and honest communication, being consistent in their behaviour, and creating a safe space for vulnerability, couples can strengthen their bond and deepen their connection. This guide has provided tips and strategies for building trust between lovers and helped couples create a strong foundation for their relationship. It's important to remember that building and maintaining trust takes time and effort, and it's a continuous process.

TAKEAWAYS

Key actions to building trust in a romantic relationship:

Communication: Open, honest, and regular communication is the foundation of trust.

Keeping promises: Following through on commitments builds trust and shows reliability.

Being transparent: Sharing thoughts, feelings, and actions builds mutual understanding and trust.

Respecting boundaries: Respecting your partner's personal space, time, and opinions fosters trust.

Being forgiving: Being able to forgive mistakes and move past conflicts shows understanding and strengthens trust.

Honesty: Being truthful and avoiding dishonesty in all aspects of the relationship builds trust and respect.

Saying "I love you" repeatedly have several benefits:

Reinforces emotional bond: The emotional connection between spouses is strengthened and the sense of love and devotion is reinforced by frequent displays of affection.

Increases intimacy: Saying "I love you" regularly creates an intimate environment where partners feel comfortable and appreciated.

Increases happiness: The act of expressing love can bring happiness to both partners and boost their overall well-being.

Fosters trust: Regularly expressing love and affection can increase trust and build a stronger foundation for the relationship.

Prevents misunderstandings: By often expressing their love, spouses may steer clear of misinterpretation and misunderstandings.

Positive Actions for Building Trust

Here are some actions you can take to build and reinforce trust in your relationship:

Keep your promises: When you make a promise to your partner, do your best to follow through on it.

Be transparent: Be open and honest about your thoughts, feelings, and actions.

Be supportive: Listen to your partner, offer encouragement and support, and help them through difficult times.

Apologize sincerely: When you make a mistake, apologize sincerely and take steps to make things right.

Show appreciation: Express your gratitude and appreciation for your partner regularly.

The Power of Small Acts of Kindness

Small acts of kindness can go a long way in building trust and strengthening a relationship. Simple gestures like bringing your partner breakfast in bed, surprising them with a special gift, or taking care of a task they've been dreading can make a big impact.

Overall, saying "I love you" repeatedly is important in maintaining and strengthening relationships, increasing happiness and intimacy, and fostering trust.

Printed in Great Britain
by Amazon